Hydesville

The Story of the Rochester Knockings, Which Proclaimed the Advent of Modern Spiritualism

by Thomas Olman Todd

Originally published in 1905.

DEDICATED TO DAISY.

A creature not too bright or good

For human nature's daily food,

For transient sorrows, simple wiles,

Praise, blame, love, kisses, tears and smiles.

—Wordsworth.

"Some secret truths from learned pride concealed,

To maids alone and children are revealed:

What though no credit doubting wits may give,

The fair and innocent shall still believe."

—Pope.

"Rightly viewed, no meanest object is insignificant; all objects are as windows, through which the philosophic eye looks into infinitude itself."—Carlyle.

"Rivers from bubbling springs

Have rise at first, and great from abject things."

—Middleton.

PREFACE.

The interesting events narrated in this book which occurred at Hydesville, in the house of the Fox Family, are those by which Modern Spiritualism made its advent into this world as a new revelation in spiritual matters.

History is not without its reliable records of similar phenomena, but, just as many scientific men have experimented and stopped short of the gateway of the actual discovery of Nature's secrets, so, many who came in contact with phenomena similar to those of Hydesville whilst being mystified as to the meaning of the operating power, stopped short of the actual discovery that "It can see as well as hear." Notably in the case of the disturbances at Mr. Mompesson's house at Tedworth (1661—1663) and Mr. Wesley's parsonage at Epworth (1716—1717).

The early literature of the Spiritualist Movement is replete with most interesting records of phenomena of bewildering variety, but during the past twenty years the demand for literature on this absorbing subject has taken a more philosophic turn. The phenomena are admittedly real. The philosophy is the subject of debate, hence these early records are fast going out of print and becoming difficult to obtain.

Some few years ago, when the writer paid what proved to be his last visit to Mrs. Emma Hardinge Britten, he was deeply impressed with her desire that the early history of the Spiritualist Movement, for which she spent the greater part of her industrious life, and with which she had been so intimately connected, should not be allowed to pass into oblivion, and that at least the story of HYDESVILLE should be published in a handy form and at a reasonable price. For this purpose she presented him with what appeared to be her only remaining copy of her invaluable historical work "Modern American Spiritualism," and requested him to undertake that duty.

The incidents recorded in the following pages are based chiefly on the information given in the work mentioned above, and considerable use is made of the actual words and sentences penned by Mrs. Britten; these are given without quotation marks. Some portions however have been re-written to adapt them to the requirements of the present book, whilst a few other facts have been gathered from various sources, chiefly Robert Dale Owen's "Footfalls on the Boundary of Another World." Both Mrs. Britten and Mr. Owen were personally acquainted with the Fox family and many of the persons incidentally mentioned in connection with the phenomena at HYDESVILLE—a fact which gives superior weight to their records.

T. O. T.

Sunderland, 1905.

Manchester,

December 5th, 1897.

Mr. T. O. Todd.

Dear Sir,

Having been a sad invalid since June of this year, and still suffering, I do not quite remember whether I have or not written to you on the subject to which I desire to devote this poor scrawl. If I have not done so hitherto—permit me to say,—altho' I have been obliged from severe illness to suspend my platform work and writings, I am as much interested in the earnest desire to help the progress of Spiritualism as I have been in my long years of past devotion to that cause.

In consequence of my sad illness I have been obliged to refuse my kind American Friends' urgent invitation to attend their Grand Celebration at Rochester, N.Y., next June.

I am most anxious to do something for our noble cause, [enquirers] will necessarily want to have some special accounts of the first opening of the Spiritual Movement and the history of the poor Fox Family and their immediate connection with the famous "Rochester Knockings." All this I, who knew the Fox Family and all the circumstances of the case personally and intimately, have written and published in full detail in my widely circulated work "Modern American Spiritualism."—But this work consists of 560 pages, and tho' bought by thousands of American

Spiritualists, I should not know in England where to turn to find a copy except in my own bookcase.

Now what I propose is this: In the first hundred pages is the full and entire history of the movement; the life and labours of A. J. Davis,—the life, sufferings, and bitter persecutions of the poor Foxes, and all their early trials; friends, foes, and all connected with them. Why cannot you . . . take those hundred pages, condense them, and make a splendid pamphlet of them?

Sincerely yours,

EMMA HARDINGE BRITTEN.

SPIRIT RAPPINGS.

(This poem will be found set to music in
the "Spiritual Songster.")

Rap, rap, rap! Rap, rap, rap! Rap, rap, rap!

Who is it rapping to-night?

Only invisible friends,

Come from those chambers whose light

Radiantly earth-ward descends,

Those whose dear forms you have covered from sight,

And mark'd by a marble shaft solemn and white,

Have come from the land where their life bloom'd anew,

And lo! by those raps they are talking to you.

Rap, rap, rap! Rap, rap, rap! Rap, rap, rap!

Daintiest fingers of air

Wake the most delicate sound

Rapping on table or chair,

Lov'd ones of earth gather round

Making us know that our lov'd ones have come,

Come back to our hearts, and their dear earthly home,

Forget they will never, thro' glory bath'd years,

How lonely they left us in sadness and tears.

Rap, rap, rap! Rap, rap, rap! Rap, rap, rap!

Guests we would honour are here!

Hear the light rappings, and know

Visiting Angels are near,

Greeting their earth friends below!

Oh, bid them welcome, in garments of white,

To hearts which are pure and illumin'd with light;

They wander at will o'er two wonderful lands,

Oh, list to their counsels, and give them your hands.

Rap, rap, rap! Rap, rap, rap! Rap, rap, rap!

Lov'd ones are rapping to-night;

Heaven seems not far away;

Death's sweeping river is bright,

Soft is the sheen of its spray.

Magical changes those rappings have wrought,

Sweet hope to the hopeless their patter has brought,

And death is bridg'd over with amaranth flow'rs:

Blest Spirits come back from their bright homes to ours.

—Emma R. Tuttle.

CHAPTER I.

The birth-places of the greatest of the world's social, political, and religious reformations have generally been of insignificant and lowly aspect, and apparently under the most inauspicious circumstances for producing any great effect upon mankind. The Babe of the lowly manger becomes the Spiritual King of millions of human hearts and souls, and the "Wood Hut" becomes the gateway through which Holy Ministers of Light, from their world of Truth and Beauty, send the evidence of man's immortality, through the instrumentality of a child, to the weary worn pilgrims of earth, who, praying for the "touch of a vanish'd hand, and the sound of a voice that is still," welcome with joyful hearts the Spirit message "WE STILL LIVE."

The scene of the manifestations dealt with in the following pages, was a small wooden homestead, one of a cluster of houses like itself, in the little village of Hydesville, near to the town of Newark, Wayne County, New York (being so called after Dr. Hyde, an old settler, whose son was the proprietor of the house in question). The place not being directly accessible from a railroad, was lonely and unmarked by those tokens of progress that the locomotive generally leaves in its track, hence it was the last spot where a scene of fraud and deception could find a possibility of a successful execution. The house was a humble frame dwelling fronting south, consisting of two fair-size parlours opening into each other, east of these a bedroom and a buttery or pantry, opening into one of the sitting rooms; and a stairway between the buttery and the bedroom leading from the sitting room up to the half storey above and from the buttery down to the cellar.

This humble dwelling had been selected as a temporary residence during the erection of another house in the country, by Mr. John D. Fox, who, with his family, soon afterwards became so prominently identified with the phenomena which have since become world famous. Their little dwelling, though so small and simply furnished as to leave no shadow of opportunity for concealment or trick, was the residence of honest piety and rural simplicity. All who ever knew them bore witness to the unimpeachable character of the good mother, while the integrity of the simple-minded farmers who were father and brother to the sisters who have since become so celebrated as the "Rochester Knockers" stands proved beyond all question.

The ancestors of Mr. Fox were Germans, the name being originally "Voss"; but both he and Mrs. Fox were native born. In Mrs. Fox's family, French by origin and Rutan by name, several individuals had evinced the power of second sight,—her maternal grandmother (Margaret Ackerman) who resided at Long Island, had frequent perceptions of coming events; so vivid were these presentiments that she frequently followed phantom funerals to the grave as if they were real.

Mrs. Fox's sister also, Mrs. Elizabeth Higgins, had similar power. On one occasion, in the year 1823, the two sisters, then residing in New York, proposed to go to Sodus by canal. But one morning Elizabeth said, "We shall not make this trip by water." "Why so?" her sister asked. "Because I dreamed last night that we travelled by land, and there was a strange person with us. In my dream, too, I thought we came to Mott's tavern on the Beech Woods, and that they could not admit us because Mrs. Mott lay dying in the house. I know it will all come true." "Very likely indeed!" her sister replied, "for last year, when we passed there, Mr.

Mott's wife lay dead in the house." "You will see. He must have married again and he will lose his second wife." Every particular came to pass as Mrs. Higgins had predicted. Mrs. Johnson, a stranger, whom at the time of the dream they had not seen, did go with them, they made the journey by land and were refused admittance into Mott's tavern for the very cause assigned in the dream.

The family of Mr. and Mrs. Fox consisted of six children, but at the time of the manifestations the house was occupied by Mr. and Mrs. Fox and their two youngest children only, Margaretta, aged twelve, and Kate, aged nine years. These details, insignificant as they may now appear, are due alike to the family and posterity. When the future of this wonderful movement shall have become matter of history and antiquity, if not reverence for spiritual truth, and shall induce mankind to follow the example of their ancestors and label the records "sacred," the names now sunk in obscurity and masked by slander may perchance be engraved in monuments of bronze and marble, and the incidents now deemed too slight for notice become reverenced as "Holy Writ." These changes of chance and time have happened before; if history repeats itself they will occur again. It was reserved to this family to be the instruments of communicating to the world this most singular affair. They were the ones who first, as if by accident, found out that there was an INTELLIGENCE MANIFESTED EVEN IN THE RAPPING, which at first appeared nothing more than an annoying and unaccountable noise.

In a publication of the early investigations connected with this house, entitled: "A Report of the Mysterious Noises heard in the house of Mr. John D. Fox, in Hydesville, Arcadia, Wayne County, authenticated by the certificates and confirmed by the statements of the citizens of that place and vicinity," we find that some disturbances had affected the house before the Fox family came to live there. In the year 1843-4, the farm was occupied by a Mr. and Mrs. Bell, who, during the last three months of their stay were joined by a young girl—Lucretia Pulver, who sometimes worked for them, and at other times boarded with them and went to school, she being about fifteen years old.

According to the statement of Lucretia, called forth by subsequent investigations, a pedlar called at the house one afternoon whom Mrs. Bell seemed to recognise as an acquaintance. He was a man about thirty years of age, dressed in a black frock coat, light trousers and vest, and carried with him a pack of goods containing dress material and other draperies.

Shortly after the arrival of the pedlar, Mrs. Bell called the girl to say that she could not afford to keep her any longer, and that as she was going to the next village the same afternoon, she might pack her clothes and they would go together. Before going, Lucretia chose from the pedlar's pack a piece of delaine, asking him to leave it at her father's house; this he promised to do the next day. Mrs. Bell and Lucretia then left the house, the pedlar and Mr. Bell remained behind, the former apparently having decided to stay there for the day. The pedlar did not call at Lucretia's father's house next day in fulfilment of his promise to do so, nor, in fact, was he ever seen again, a circumstance which should be borne in mind when the sequel to this story is under consideration.

About three days afterwards, much to the girl's surprise, Mrs. Bell sent for Lucretia to return to her again. She did so, and from that time she began to hear noises and knockings in her bedroom, the same room which was afterwards occupied by Mr. and Mrs. Fox. On one occasion, when Mr. and Mrs. Bell were away from home at Lock Berlin, and Lucretia had to remain in the house, she sent for her young brother and a girl friend named Aurelia Losey to stay in the house with her. During the night they all heard noises which they declared sounded like the footsteps of a man passing from the bedroom to the buttery, then down the cellar stairs, traversing the cellar for a short time and then suddenly stopping. They were all very much frightened and got up to fasten the doors and windows, but were scarcely able to sleep the remainder of the night.

About a week after the visit of the pedlar to the house, Lucretia having occasion to go down into the cellar, stumbled and fell into a hole filled with soft soil, this somewhat frightened her and caused her to scream for assistance. Mrs. Bell coming to her rescue, Lucretia asked what Mr. Bell had been doing in the cellar that it was all "dug up." Mrs. Bell replied that "the holes were only rat holes," and a few nights afterwards Lucretia observed that Mr. Bell was busy for some time in the cellar filling up the "rat holes" with earth which he carried there himself.

During the remainder of the period in which the house was occupied by the Bell family, the sounds continued to be heard, not only by Lucretia but by Mrs. Bell. Lucretia's mother, Mrs. Pulver, was a frequent visitor at the house, and on one occasion in particular, after the foregoing events, when she called upon Mrs. Bell, she found the latter quite ill from want of rest, and on enquiring the cause, Mrs. Bell declared she was "sick of her life," and that she frequently "heard the footsteps of a man traversing the house all night."

CHAPTER II.

A few months after these events happened the Bells left the neighbourhood, and the house became tenanted by a Mr. and Mrs. Weekman, who lived there about eighteen months, and left in the year 1847. Mr. Weekman's statement respecting the noises he heard was to the effect that one evening when he was about to retire for the night, he heard a rapping on the outside door, and, what was rather unusual for him, instead of familiarly bidding them "come in," stepped to the door and opened it. He had no doubt of finding some one who wished to come in, but to his surprise found no one there. He stepped out and looked around, supposing that some person was imposing on him, he could discover no one, and went back into the house. After a short time he heard the rapping again, and stepped up and held on to the latch, so that he might ascertain if any one had taken that means to annoy him. The rapping was repeated, the door opened instantly, but no one was in sight. Mr. Weekman states that he could feel the jar of the door very plainly when the rapping was heard. As he opened the door he sprang out and went around the house, but no one was in sight, nor could he find trace of any intruder.

They were frequently afterwards disturbed by strange and unaccountable noises. One night Mrs. Weekman heard what she deemed to be the footsteps of someone walking in the cellar. Another night Mr. Weekman and his wife were disturbed by hearing a scream from their child, a girl about eight years of age,—this happened at midnight,—they went to her and she told them that something like a hand passed over her face and head; it seemed cold, and so badly had she been frightened that it was some time before she could be induced to tell her parents the cause of her alarm, nor would she consent to sleep in the same room for several nights afterwards.

All this might have happened, and been only the idle fabric of a child's dream, the Weekman family might have imagined what they gave out as fact, and we should be inclined to believe that such was the case, if we had not the most conclusive evidence that such manifestations were quite common, not only in this house, but in various others where similarly strange things have happened.

CHAPTER III.

"Know well my soul, God's hand controls

Whate'er thou fearest."

From the time the Fox family entered the house at Hydesville, about December, 1847, they were incessantly disturbed by similar noises to those heard by Lucretia Pulver and the Weekmans. During the next month however (January, 1848) the noises began to assume the character of slight knockings heard at night in the bedroom; sometimes appearing to sound from the cellar beneath. At first Mrs. Fox sought to persuade herself this might be the hammering of a shoemaker in a house hard by, sitting up late at work. But further observation showed that the sounds originated in the house. For not only did the knockings become more distinct, and not only were they heard first in one part of the house, then in another, but the family remarked that these raps, even when not very loud, often caused a motion, tremulous rather than a sudden jar, of the bedsteads and chairs—sometimes of the floor; a motion which was quite perceptible to the touch when a hand was laid on the chairs, which was sometimes sensibly felt at night in the slightly oscillating motion of the bed, and which was occasionally perceived as a sort of vibration even when standing on the floor. After a time also, the noises varied in their character, sounding occasionally like distinct footfalls in the different rooms.

In the month of February, the noises became so distinct and continuous that their rest was broken night after night, and they were all becoming worn out in their efforts to discover the cause of the annoyances. These disturbances were not confined to sounds merely,—once something heavy, as if a dog, seemed to lie on the feet of the children; but it was gone before the mother could come to their aid. Another time (this was late in March) Kate felt as if a cold hand was on her face. Occasionally too, the bedclothes were pulled during the night. Finally chairs were moved from their places. The disturbances, which had been limited to occasional knockings throughout February and March, gradually increased towards the close of the latter month, both in loudness and frequency. Mr. Fox and his wife got up night after night, lit a candle, and thoroughly searched every nook and corner of the house; but without any result. They discovered nothing. When the raps came on a door, Mr. Fox would stand, ready to open the door the instant the raps were repeated. Though he opened the door immediately there was no one to be seen. Nor did he or Mrs. Fox obtain any clue as to the cause of the trouble, notwithstanding all the efforts they made and the precautions they exercised.

The only circumstance which seemed to suggest the possibility of trickery or of mistake was, that these various unexplained occurrences never happened in daylight, and thus notwithstanding the strangeness of the thing, when morning came they began to think it must have been the fancy of the night. Not being given to superstition, they clung, throughout several weeks of annoyance, to the idea that some natural explanation of these seemingly mysterious events would at last appear, nor did they abandon this hope till the night of

FRIDAY, MARCH 31st, 1848,

a date which was destined to be indelibly imprinted on the minds of the coming generations as the daybreak of a new era in the spiritual development of humanity, a date which has since been regularly observed as marking the advent of the greatest spiritual revelation of modern times, and recognised as the anniversary of the Spiritualist movement in all parts of the world.

CHAPTER IV.

The day had been cold and stormy, with snow on the ground. In the course of the afternoon, David, a son of Mr. and Mrs. Fox, came to visit his parents from his farm about three miles distant. Mrs. Fox then first recounted to him the particulars of the annoyances they had endured; for until now they had been little disposed to communicate these to any one. He listened to her with a smiling face. "Well mother," he said, "I advise you not to say a word about it to the neighbours. When you find it out it will be one of the simplest things in the world." And in that belief he returned to his own home.

Wearied out by a succession of sleepless nights and of fruitless attempts to penetrate the mystery, the Fox family retired on that Friday evening very early to rest, hoping for a respite from the disturbances that harassed them. But they were doomed to disappointment. The parents had had the children's beds removed into their own bedroom, and strictly enjoined them not to talk of the noises even if they heard them. But scarcely had the mother seen them safely in bed, and was retiring to rest herself, when the children cried out "Here they are again." The mother chid them and lay down, but as though in rebuke of her apparent indifference, they were on this occasion louder and more pertinacious than ever. Rest was impossible. The children kept up a continuous chatter, sitting up in bed to listen to the sounds. Mr. Fox tried the windows and doors, to discover, if possible, the source of the annoyance. The night being windy it suggested itself to him that it might be the sashes rattling, but all in vain; the raps continued and were evidently answering the noise occasioned by the father shaking the windows, as if in mockery.

At length the youngest child, Kate—who in her guileless innocence had become familiar with the invisible knocker, until she was more amused than alarmed at its presence—merrily exclaimed: "Here, Mr. Split-foot, do as I do." The effect was instantaneous: the invisible rapper responded by imitating the number of her movements. She then made a given number of motions with her finger and thumb in the air, but without noise, and her astonishment was re-doubled to find that these movements were seen by the invisible rapper, for a corresponding number of knocks were immediately given to her noiseless motions, whilst from her lips as though but in childish jest and transport at her new discovery there sprang to life the words which revealed the sublimest Spiritual Truth of modern times: "Only look mother

IT CAN SEE AS WELL AS HEAR."

Words which have since become a text which Doctors, Professors, sceptics and scoffers have tried to crush out of existence—and ignominiously failed, but which on the other hand have brought comfort, solace, and permanent joy to the hearts of hundreds of thousands—nay, millions surely,—of earth's weary pilgrims. Words which declared a truth since tested by every possible subtlety and sophistry which the ingenuity of man could suggest or devise, but which has stood firmly through every ordeal. Words which declare a truth that has already become the firm foundation of faith for an ever progressive Spiritual Church, made up of almost every nation of the earth, and embracing adherents from every rank of philosophic, scientific, religious and social life, which, moreover, reveals its own attributes to the child and the philosopher alike, and provides the missing link between a finite material world and a world of infinite spiritual possibilities by proving the continuity of life.

CHAPTER V.

Happily for the momentous work which the spiritual telegraphers had undertaken to initiate in this humble dwelling, the first manifestations did not appeal to the high and learned of the earth, but to the plain common-sense of an honest farmer's wife, and suggested that whatever could see, hear, and intelligently respond to relevant queries, must have in it something in common with humanity; and thus Mrs. Fox continued her investigations. Addressing the viewless rapper she said "count ten;" the raps obeyed. "How old is my daughter Margaret?" then "Kate?" Both questions were distinctly and correctly rapped out. Mrs. Fox then asked "How many children have I?" Seven, was the reply; this however proved to be wrong for she had only six living. She repeated her question and was again answered by seven raps; suddenly she cried "How many have I living?" Six raps responded. "How many dead?" a single knock; and both these answers proved correct. To the next question, "Are you a man that knocks?" there was no response; but "Are you a spirit?" elicited firm and distinctive responsive knocks.

Emboldened by her success, Mrs. Fox continued her enquiries and ascertained by raps that the messages were coming from what purported to be the Spirit of an injured man who had been murdered for his money. To the question how old he was, there came thirty-one distinct raps. He also gave them to understand that he was a married man, and had left a wife and five children; that his wife was dead, and had been dead two years. After ascertaining so much, she asked the question "Will the noise continue if I call in some neighbours?" The answer was by rapping in the affirmative.

At first they called in their nearest neighbours, who came thinking they would have a hearty laugh at the family for being frightened—but when the first neighbour came in and found that the noise, whatever it might be, could tell the age of herself as well as others, and give correct answers to questions on matters of which the family of Mr. Fox was quite ignorant, she concluded that there was something beside a subject of ridicule and laughter in these unseen but audible communications. These neighbours insisted on calling others who came, and after investigation were as much confounded as at first.

The reader must endeavour to picture to himself the scene which followed the introduction of the neighbours to this weird and most novel court of inquiry. Imagine the place to be an humble cottage in a remote and obscure hamlet; the judge and jurors, simple unsophisticated rustics; and the witness an invisible, unknown being, a denizen of a world of whose very existence mankind has been ignorant; acting by laws mysterious and inconceivable, in modes utterly beyond all human control or comprehension, and breaking through what has been deemed the dark and eternal seal of death, to reveal the long-hidden mysteries of the grave, and drag to the light secrets which not even the fabled silence of the grave could longer hide away. Those who have been accustomed to dream of death as the end of all whom its shadowy portals inclose, alone are prepared to appreciate the awful and startling reality of this strange scene, breaking apart, as it did, like a rope of sand, all the preconceived opinions of countless ages on the existence and destiny of the living dead.

Those who have become familiar with the revealments of the spirit circle will only smile at the consternation evoked in this rustic party by the now familiar presence and manifestations of "the spirits," but to those who still stand in the night of superstition, deeming of all earth's countless millions as "dead," "lost," "gone," no one knows whither; never to return; to give no sign, no echo, no dim vibration from that vast gulf profound of unfathomed mystery—what a picture is that which suddenly brings them face to face with the mighty hosts of the vanished dead, all clothed in life, and girded round with a panoply of power, and light, and strength; with vivid memory of the secret wrongs deemed buried in their graves. Our cities are thronged with an unseen people who flit about us, their piercing eyes invisible to us, are scanning all our ways. The universe is teeming with them,—"THERE ARE NO DEAD,"—the air, the earth, and the sky above, are filled with a viewless host of spirit—witnesses whose messages ever declare "There is no death."

CHAPTER VI.

Amongst the investigators introduced to the household was a Mr. William Deusler, of Arcadia, an immediate neighbour of the Fox family at this time, and from his testimony we gather a great many interesting facts as to the evidence offered by the injured spirit in order that its identity could be clearly established.

Mr. Deusler had formerly lived with his father in this house, and the message that the spirit had received an injury, prompted him to ask if either he or his father had been the cause of such an injury. On receiving an assurance that they were in no way responsible, the investigation was continued, the results being here given in Mr. Deusler's own words—

"I then asked if Mr. —— [naming a person who had formerly lived in the house] had injured it, and if so, to manifest it by rapping, and it made three knocks louder than common, and at the same time the bedstead jarred more than it had done before. I then inquired if it was murdered for money, and the knocking was heard. I then requested it to rap when I mentioned the sum of money for which it was murdered. I then asked if it was one hundred, two, three or four, and when I came to five hundred the rapping was heard. All in the room said they heard it distinctly. I then asked the question if it was five hundred dollars, and the rapping was heard.

"After this, I sent over and got Artemus W. Hyde to come over. [A] He came over. I then asked over nearly the same questions as before, and got the same answers. Mr. Redfield sent after David Jewel and wife, and Mrs. Hyde also came. After they came in I asked the same questions over and got the same answers. . . . I then asked it to rap my age—the number of years of my age. It rapped thirty times. This is my age, and I do not think any one about here knew my age, except myself and family. I then told it to rap my wife's age, and it rapped thirty times, which is her exact age; several of us counted it at the same time. I then asked it to rap A. W. Hyde's age; then Mrs. A. W. Hyde's age. I then continued to ask it to rap the ages of different persons—naming them—in the room, and it did so correctly, as they all said. I then asked the number of children in the different families in the neighbourhood, and it told them correctly in the usual way, by rapping; also the number of deaths that had taken place in the different families, and it told correctly. . . .

"I then asked in regard to the time it was murdered, and in the usual way, by asking the different days of the week and the different hours of the day, learned that it was murdered on Tuesday night, about twelve o'clock. The rapping was heard only when this particular time was mentioned. When it was asked if it was murdered on a Wednesday, or Thursday, or Friday night, etc., there was no rapping. I then asked if it carried any trunk, and it rapped that it did. Then how many, and it rapped once. In the same way we ascertained that it had goods in the trunk, and that —— took them when he murdered him; and that he had a pack of goods besides. I asked if its wife was living, and it did not rap. If she was dead, and it rapped. . . . This was tried over several times and the result was always the same.

"I then tried to ascertain the first letters of its name by calling over the different letters of the alphabet. I commenced with A, and asked if it was the initial of its name; and when I asked if it was B the rapping commenced. We then tried all the other letters, but could get no answer by the usual rapping. I then asked if we could find out the whole name by reading over all the letters of the alphabet, and there was no rapping. I then reversed the question, and the rapping was heard. . . . There were a good many more questions asked on that night by myself and others which I do not now remember. They were all readily answered in the same way. I staid in the house until about twelve o'clock and then came home. Mr. Redfield and Mr. Fox staid in the house that night.

"Saturday night I went over again about seven o'clock. The house was full of people when I got there. They said it had been rapping some time. I went into the room. It was rapping in answer to questions when I went in. . . .

"There were as many as three hundred people in and around the house at this time, I should think. Hiram Soverhill, Esq., and Volney Brown asked it questions while I was there, and it rapped in answer to them.

"I went over again on Sunday between one and two o'clock p.m. I went into the cellar with several others, and had them all leave the house over our heads; and then I asked, if there had been a man buried in the cellar, to manifest it by rapping or any other noise or sign. The moment I asked the question there was a sound like the falling of a stick about a foot long and half an inch through, on the floor in the bedroom over our heads. It did not seem to rebound at all; there was but one sound. I then asked Stephen Smith to go right up and examine the room, and see if he could discover the cause of the noise. He came back and said he could discover nothing; that there was no one in the room, or in that part of the house. I then asked two more questions, and it rapped in the usual way. We all went upstairs and made a thorough search, but could find nothing.

"I then got a knife and fork, and tried to see if I could make the same noise by dropping them, but I could not. This was all I heard on Sunday. There is only one floor, or partition, or thickness between the bedroom and the cellar; no place where anything could be secreted to make the noise. When this noise was heard in the bedroom I could feel a slight tremulous motion or jar. . . .

"On Monday night I heard this noise again, and asked the same questions I did before and got the same answers. This is the last time I have heard any rapping. I can in no way account for this singular noise which I and others have heard. It is a mystery to me which I am unable to solve. . . .

"I lived in the same house about seven years ago, and at that time never heard any noises of the kind in and about the premises. I have understood from Johnston and others who have lived there before —— moved there, that there were no such sounds heard there while they occupied the house. I never believed in haunted houses, or heard or saw anything but what I could account for before.

(Signed),

WILLIAM DEUSLER."

"April 12, 1848."

To the same effect is the testimony of the following persons, whose certificates were published in a pamphlet by E. E. Lewis, Esq., of Canandaigua, New York, namely: John D. Fox, Walter Scotten, Elizabeth Jewel, Lorren Tenney, James Bridger, Chauncey P. Losey, Benjamin F. Clark, Elizabeth Fox, Vernelia Culver, William D. Storer, Marvin P. Losey, David S. Fox, and Mary Redfield.

FOOTNOTE:

[A] The son of the proprietor of the house at Hydesville.

CHAPTER VII.

The news of the mysterious rappings continued to spread abroad, and the house was filled with anxious seekers for the unknown and invisible visitor. Up to this time the noises had only been heard at night, but on Sunday morning, April 2nd, the sounds were first heard in the daytime, and by any who could get into the house. It has been estimated that at one time there were about five hundred people gathered around the house, so great was the excitement at the commencement of these strange occurrences.

On the Monday following, Mr. Fox and others commenced digging in the cellar, but as the house was built on low ground and in the vicinity of a stream then much swollen by rains, it was not surprising that they were baffled by the influx of water at the distance of three feet down. In the summer of 1848, when the ground was dry and the water lowered, the digging again commenced, when they found a plank, a vacant place or hole, some bits of crockery, which seemed to have been a washbowl, traces of charcoal, quicklime, some human hair, bones (declared on examination by a surgeon to be human), including a portion of a skull, but no connected skull was found.

[Interesting facts relating to the missing portions of the human body were announced in the public newspapers as recently as December, 1904, for which see Appendix.]

Such were the results of the examination of the cellar; such the only corroborative evidences obtained of the truth of the spirit's tale of untimely death. The presence of human remains in the cellar proves that someone was buried there, and the quicklime and charcoal testify to the fact that attempts were made to secretly dispose of the body of the victim.

The Fox family did not immediately quit the scene of this mysterious haunting, but remained to witness still more astounding phenomena. The furniture was frequently moved about; the girls were often touched by hard cold hands; doors were opened and shut with violence; their beds were so violently shaken that they were obliged to "camp out" as they termed it, on the ground; their bedclothes were dragged from them, and the very floor and house made to rock as in an earthquake. Night after night they would be appalled by hearing a sound like a death struggle, the gurgling of the throat, a sudden thud as of something falling, the dragging as of a helpless body across the room and down the cellar stairs, the digging of a grave, nailing of boards, and the filling up as of a new made grave. These sounds have subsequently been produced by request, and spontaneously also, in the presence of many persons assembled in circles at Rochester.

It was perceived that "the spirits" seemed to select or require the presence of the two younger girls of the family for the production of the sounds, and though these had been made without them, especially on the night of the 31st of March, when all the members of the family save Mr. Fox were absent from the house, still as curiosity prompted them to close observation and conversation with the invisible power, it was clear that the manifestations became more powerful in the presence of Kate, the youngest daughter, than with any one else.

As the house was continually thronged with curious inquirers, and the time, comfort and peace of the family were consumed with these harassing disturbances, besides the most absurd though injurious suspicions being cast upon them, they endeavoured to baffle the haunters by sending Kate to reside with her eldest sister, Mrs. Fish, at Rochester; but no sooner had she gone than the manifestations re-commenced with more force than ever, in the presence of Margaretta. In course of time Mrs. Fox, with both her daughters, went to live in Rochester, but neither change of place nor house, nor yet the separation of the family, afforded them any relief from the disturbances that evidently attached themselves to persons rather than places as formerly.

Although the Fox family had for months striven to banish the power that tormented them, praying with all the fervour of true Methodism to be released from it, and enduring fear, loss and anxiety in its continuance, the report of its persistence began to spread abroad, causing a rain of persecutions to fall upon them from all quarters. Old friends looked coldly on them, and strangers circulated the most atrocious slanders at their expense.

Mrs. Fish, the eldest sister, who was a teacher of music in Rochester, began to lose her pupils, and whilst the blanching of the poor mother's hair in a single week bore testimony to the mental tortures which supra-mundane terrors and mundane cruelties had heaped upon them, the world was taunting them with imposture and with originating the very manifestations which were destroying their health, peace of mind, and good name. They had solicited the advice of their much-respected friend, Isaac Post, a highly esteemed Quaker citizen of Rochester, and at his suggestion succeeded in communicating by raps with the invisible power, through the alphabet (an attempt had been previously made but without success). Telegraphic numbers were given to signify "Yes" or "No," "Doubtful," etc., and sentences were spelled out by which they learned the astounding facts that not only "Charles Rosna" the murdered pedlar, but hosts of spirits, good and bad, high and low, could under certain conditions not understood, and impossible for mortals yet to comprehend, communicate with earth; that such communication was produced through the forces of spiritual magnetism, in chemical affinity; that the varieties of magnetism in different individuals afforded "medium power" to some, and denied it to others; that the magnetic relations necessary to produce phenomena were very subtle, liable to disturbance and singularly susceptible to the influence of the mental emotions. In addition to communications purporting thus to explain the object and something of the modus operandi of the communion, numerous spirit friends of the family, and also of those who joined in their investigations, gladdened the hearts of their astonished relatives by direct and unlooked-for tests of their presence. They came spelling out their names, ages and various tokens of identity correctly, and proclaiming the joyful tidings that they all "still lived," "still loved," and with the tenderness of human affection and the wisdom of a higher sphere of existence, watched over and guided the beloved ones who had mourned them as dead, with all the gracious ministry of guardian angels.

CHAPTER VIII.

But redolent of joy and consolation as is the intercourse with beloved friends, at this time when orderly communion has succeeded doubtful experiment, it must not be supposed that any such harmonious results characterised the initiatory proceedings of the spiritual movement which now made its advent in Rochester.

Within and without the dwellings of the medium, all was fear, consternation, doubt, and anxiety. Fanatical religionists of different sects had forced themselves into the family gatherings, and the wildest scenes of rant, cant, and absurdity often ensued. Opinions of the most astounding nature were hazarded concerning the object of this movement; some determining that it was a "millennium" and looking for the speedy reign of a personal Messiah and the equally speedy destruction of the wicked.

It must not be supposed that the clergy were idle spectators of the tumultuous wave that was sweeping over the city. On the contrary, several of them called on Mrs. Fox with offers to "exorcise the spirits," and when they found their attempts futile, and that though the spirits would rap in chorus to the "amens" with which they concluded their incantations, they were otherwise unmoved by these reverend performances, they generally ended by proclaiming abroad that the family were "in league with the evil one," or the "authors of a vile imposture."

Honourable exceptions, however, were found to this cowardly and unchristian course, and amongst these was the Rev. A. H. Jervis, a Methodist minister of Rochester, in whose family remarkable manifestations occurred of the same character as in that of the Foxes, and whose appreciation of the beauty and worth of the communications he received, several of his published letters bear witness of. Mr. Lyman Granger, Rev. Charles Hammond, Deacon Hale, and several other families of wealth and influence, both in Rochester and the surrounding towns, also began to experience similar phenomena in their own households, while the news came from all quarters, extending as far as Cincinnati and St. Louis, West, and Maine, Massachusetts, Pennsylvania, and New York, East, that the mysterious rappings and other phases of what is now called "medium power" were rapidly spreading from town to town and State to State, in fulfilment of an assurance made in the very first of the communications to the Fox family, namely, "that these manifestations were not to be confined to them, BUT WOULD GO ALL OVER THE WORLD."

The remarkable manner in which this prophecy has been fulfilled the most casual observer will readily admit; for Spiritualism—even as a religious power—has far outstripped any other form of religion in the world in the rapidity of its growth, having reached every civilized nation and permeated every other form of belief in less than half a century.

The Fox Sisters were still called the "Rochester Knockers," the "Fox Girls," the "Rappers," and other epithets, equally foolish and obnoxious to their interests and feelings. Catherine Fox, the youngest girl, had been removed to the house of Mr. W. E. Capron, of Auburn. Mrs. Fish, though generally present when phenomena were transpiring, was not in its earliest phases conscious of being a medium. Margaretta, the other sister, was then in reality the only one through whom the manifestations appeared to proceed, when in November, 1848, the spirits, who had long been urging them to permit public investigations to be made through her mediumship, informed them by raps that "they could not always strive with them," and since they were constantly disobedient to the spirits' requests, and obviously opposed to their presence, they should leave them, and in all probability withdraw for another generation, or seek through other sources for the fulfilment of the high and holy purposes for which this spiritual outpouring had been designed. To these appeals the family were inflexible. They constantly prayed that the cup of this great bitterness "might pass from them." They did not wish to be "mediums," and abhorred the notoriety, scandal, and persecution which their fatal gift had brought them, and when warned that the spirits would leave them, they protested their delight at the announcement, and expressed their earnest desire that it might be fulfilled.

There were present at a circle, when communications of this character were made, several influential persons of the city, who had become greatly interested in the manifestations and were warm friends of the family. They could not, however, realise that the threat here implied would actually be fulfilled until the spirits, by rappings, spelled out several messages of a particularly affectionate and valedictory character. The scene became, says an eye-witness, solemn and impressive. The spirits announced that in twenty minutes they would depart, and exactly as that time expired they spelled out, "We will now bid you all farewell;" when the raps entirely ceased.

The family expressed themselves "glad to get rid of them;" the friends present vainly tried to obtain, by solicitations, made, as it would seem, to empty air, some demonstration that this beneficent and wonderful visitation had not indeed wholly ceased. All was useless. A mournful silence filled the apartment which had but a few minutes before been tenanted with angels, sounding out their messages of undying affection, tender counsel, wise instruction, and prescient warning. The spirits indeed were gone; and as one by one the depressed party separated and passed out into the silent moonlit streets of Rochester, all and each of them felt as if some great light had suddenly gone out, and life was changed to them. There was a mighty blank in space and a shadow everywhere, but spirit light came no more to illuminate the thick darkness.

A fortnight passed away, during which the former investigators called constantly on the Fox family to enquire if their spirit friends had returned. For the first few days a stoical negative was their only reply; after this, they began more and more fully to recognise the loss they had sustained. The wise counsellors were gone; the sources of strange strength and superhuman consolation were cut off. The tender, loving, wonderful presence no more flitted around their steps, cheered their meals, encouraged them in their human weakness, or guided them in their blindness. And these most wonderful and providential beings their own waywardness had driven from them. At last, then, they met their enquiring friends with showers of tears, choking sobs, and expressions of the bitterest self-reproach and regret.

On the twelfth day of this great heart-dearth, Mr. W. E. Capron, being in Rochester on business, called at the house of Mrs. Fish, with Mr. George Willets, a member of the Society of Friends, and one of their earliest spiritual investigators. On receiving the usual sorrowful reply that "the spirits had left them," Mr. Capron said: "Perhaps they will rap for us if not for you." They then entered the hall and put the usual question if the spirits would rap for them, in answer to which, and to the unspeakable delight of all present, they were greeted with a perfect shower of the much-lamented sounds.

Once more the spirits urged them to make the manifestations public. Again they reiterated the charge with solemn earnestness, and despite of the mediums' continued aversion to the task imposed upon them, the fear of a fresh and final bereavement of the inestimable boon of spirit communion prevented their continued resistance to the course proposed.

When the persons who were called upon to aid the mediums and take somewhat prominent parts in the work urged the awkwardness of the positions assigned them, the spirits only replied, "Your triumph will be so much the greater." There is no doubt that the severe warning they had just received, and the fear of its repetition, acted upon the whole party with more force than any argument that could have been used to induce their submission.

At the injunctions of the spirits a public investigation into the possibility of communion between the world of spirits and the earth they once inhabited was carried out. Magistrates, editors, and professional men were the judges, and enlightened American citizens the jury. The aim of wide-spread publicity was attained. Thousands heard and wondered at, and finally believed in spiritual communion who would never have dreamed of the subject but for the persecution and slander that was publicly directed against the "Rochester Knockers."

The records of these persecutions and slanders abound with disgraceful and painful incidents which, whilst being discreditable to the persons responsible for their propagation redound with full credit to the honour and integrity of the mediums selected by the Spirit world to be the forerunners of a new dispensation.

And thus the fiery cross, carried by the hands of unseen messengers, sped from point to point; the beacon fires lighted by invisible hands gleamed on every mountain top, and the low muffled sound of the spirit-raps that first broke the slumbers of the peaceful inhabitants of the humble tenement at Hydesville, became the clarion peal that sounded out to the millions of the Western Hemisphere, the anthem of the soul's immortality, chorused by hosts of God's bright ministering angels.

THE MAIDENS OF THE DAWNING LIGHT.

(Leah, Kate, Margaret.)

Oh, rustic little martyrs for the truth!

Whose earthly eyes so oft were dimmed with tears,

While on your cheeks the blush and bloom of youth

Was yet unsoiled by unborn struggling years.

Long years of suffering, years of holy joys,

Years of defeats and years of victories;

Years of sweet singing and of brawling noise,

Despair—but ever angel messages.

The memory of your mortal lives comes back;

Poor little girls! Why was the world so rough?

Of balm you brought there ever was a lack—
Of heavenly tidings never half enough!

Yet when to you the gentle "rappings" came,
Telling the story of immortal life,

The hungry world went crazy-mad to blame,
Accuse, defile, hunt, mob, make venomed strife.

Humble and poor as Christ was—kindly, too,
It seems so strange the thistle, hatred, grew

To whip your tender backs, with great ado,
Because you builded better than you knew.

But that is over. You have disappeared
From conflicts and from suffering, and to-day

From God's high country, we, your friends, endeared

By common aims, feel that you look this way.

Welcome, oh, heavenly sisters! See the light

Your youthful fingers kindled! How it spreads,

Lighting up places where were sin and night,

Whitening souls and shaping princely heads.

Lo! far it spreads! Beyond the rolling seas

Vast congregations celebrate the day

Your questionings unlocked death's mysteries,

And hailed the angels, who had come your way.

—Emma Rood Tuttle.

APPENDIX

A SEQUEL to the "ROCHESTER KNOCKINGS," after 56 years.

Copied from the "Banner of Light," (Boston, U.S.A.)

December 3rd, 1904.

"TRUTH CRUSHED TO EARTH WILL

RISE AGAIN."

Regardless of what the "Banner" knows of this matter, we prefer to present the following statement as given in the Boston Journal of Nov. 23. To opponents of the claims made by Spiritualists, the account may bear greater weight than if made by a Spiritualist paper. Take note that the Journal says, "an almost entire human skeleton," and not the bones of a large dog or of any four-footed animal.

Rochester, N. Y., Nov. 22, 1904.—The skeleton of the man supposed to have caused the rappings first heard by the Fox sisters in 1848 has been found in the walls of the house occupied by the sisters, and clears them from the only shadow of doubt held concerning their sincerity in the discovery of spirit communication.

The Fox sisters declared they learned to communicate with the spirit of a man, and that he told them he had been murdered and buried in the cellar. Repeated excavations failed to locate the body and thus give proof positive of their story.

The discovery was made by school children playing in the cellar of the building in Hydesville known as the "Spook house," where the Fox sisters heard the wonderful rappings. William H. Hyde, a reputable citizen of Clyde, who owns the house, made an investigation and found an almost entire human skeleton between the earth and crumbling cellar walls, undoubtedly that of the wandering pedlar whom it was claimed was murdered in the east room of the house, and whose body was hidden in the cellar.

Mr. Hyde has notified relatives of the Fox sisters and the notice of the discovery will be sent to the National Order of Spiritualists, many of whom remember having made pilgrimages to the "Spook house," as it is commonly called. The finding of the bones practically corroborates the sworn statement made by Margaret Fox, April 11, 1848. The Fox sisters claimed to have been disturbed by rappings and finally by a system of signals got into communication with the spirit.

According to Margaret Fox's statement the spirit was that of a pedlar, who described how he had been murdered in the house, his body being buried in the cellar. There were numerous witnesses to the rappings, but although the cellar had been dug up many times no traces of the body was found until the crumbling cellar walls revealed the skeleton.

The name of the murdered man, according to his revelation to the Fox sisters, was Charles Rosna, and the murderer a man named Beck. In 1847 the house was occupied by

Michael Weekman, a poor laborer. He and his family became troubled by these mysterious rappings, which followed in succession at different intervals, especially during the night. The family became so broken by fear and loss of sleep that they vacated the house. On Dec. 11, the Fox family moved in and two months later the rappings were resumed and the family became frightened. Finally Margaret and Cathie grew bold and asked questions which were answered, revealing the murder.

FROM HYDESVILLE.

The "Sunflower," December, 1904, says: "The following bit of information was transmitted hitherward, which, if confirmed, will create additional interest in Spiritualism, although, by no means confirming the latter, as that does not rest exclusively on the phenomena at Hydesville; for since then we have had many additional phenomena, as the varied physical phases, materialisation, slate-writing and drawing, painting, levitation, passing of matter through matter, trance-speaking, clairvoyance, psychometric reading, and numerous other modes of communicating with the spirit world. The correspondent says: William H. Hyde, who recently found the arm and leg bones of a human being at the old Fox homestead, made another search in the cellar where the bones were first exposed by the caving in of the inside cellar wall. Mr. Hyde discovered all the other important bones except the skull. The latter corroborates the statement as made in the history of the first rappings, a work entitled, 'The Missing Link in Spiritualism.'"

Note by Editor.—Attention is drawn to the fact that a portion of the skull (which the foregoing report declares to be missing) was discovered during the digging operations at the time of the "Knockings"—1848.

Made in United States
Orlando, FL
12 August 2024